Keeping a

Northcott School

Written by Jeanne Willis

Oh, what a whopper!

Q: Are elephants good pets?
A: No. Elephants are too big!

no trunk

trunk

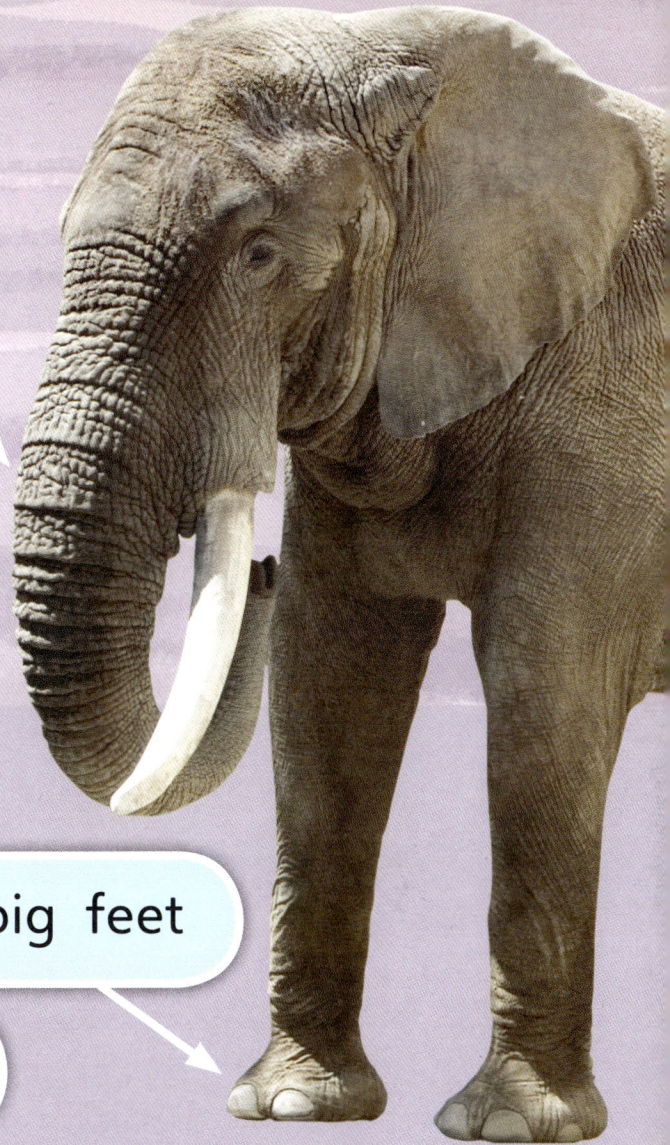

big feet

little feet

Q: Which pet is good to keep?

A: A hamster is good to keep.

Whizz!

Q: Which hamsters are good pets?

A: Hamsters that whizz up and
down are good pets.

Whoosh!

Whatever you do, do not
get an elephant that
whizzes up and down!

bed

Q: Can a hamster sleep in my bed?

A: No. A hamster sleeps in a hamster bed.

Q: Can an elephant sleep in a
   hamster bed?
A: No. An elephant is too big!

Q: What bedding is good for hamsters?
A: Shredded bedding is a good nest.

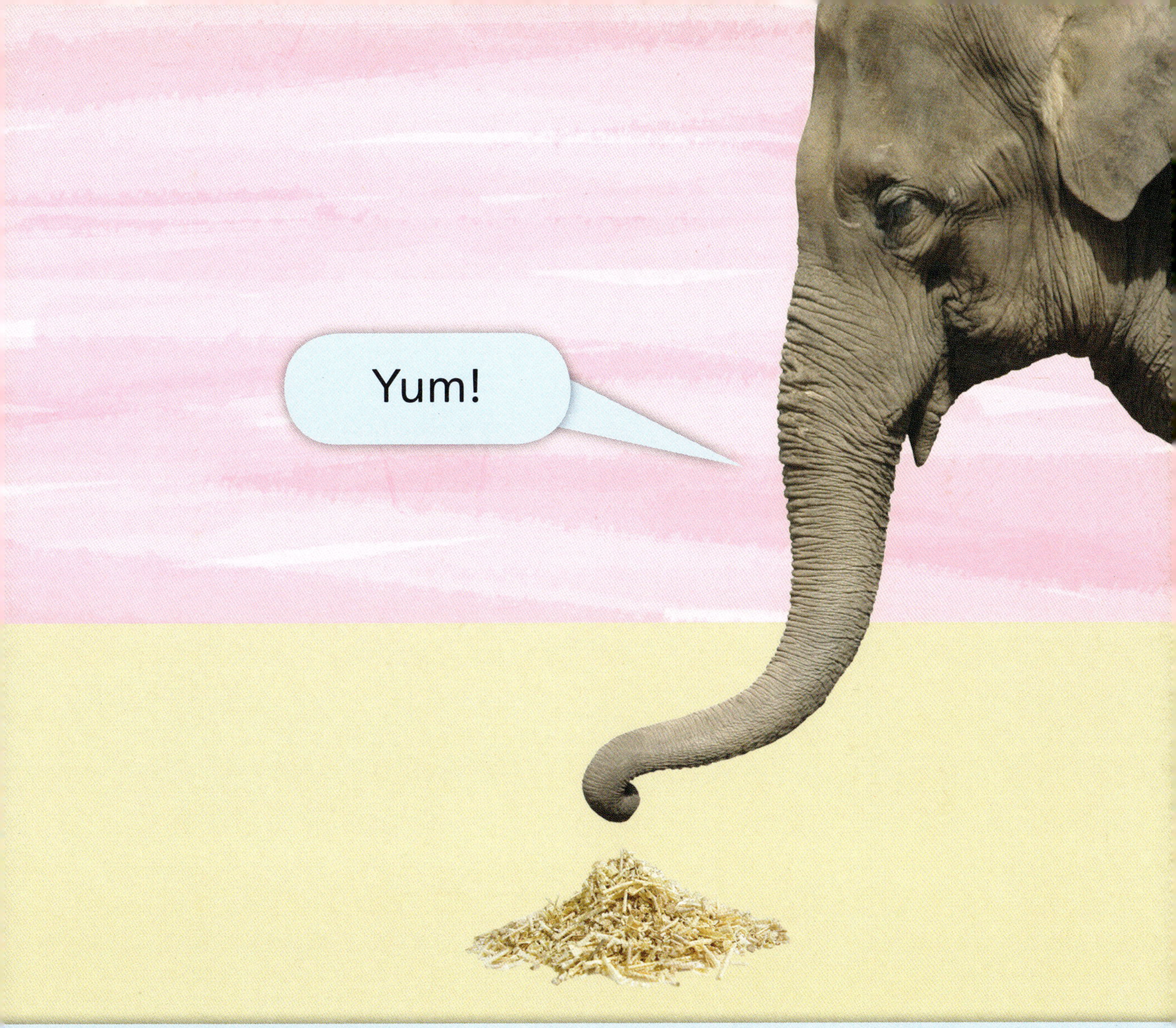

Whatever you do, do not let
an elephant have a hamster's bed.

little hamster mess

bedding

Q: Do hamsters need lots of bedding?
A: Yes. They do lots of mess!

Whopping elephant mess!

Elephants do big messes.
They are not good pets!

Whizz!

wheel

Q: What do hamsters like to do?
A: They like to run in their wheels.

Whatever you do, do not let
an elephant run on wheels!

hamster mix

Q: What food is good for hamsters?
A: Hamster mix is good for hamsters.

Whopping hamster!

Whatever you do, do not feed
elephant mix to a hamster!

Q: What if you feed an elephant hamster mix?

A: It is a good little pet!